HEARTQUAKE

From the End to the Beginning

www.dorakiki.com

London.uk

Publisher ©2021 Dora & Kiki Ltd

Author ©2021 Oscar Travino

Illustrations ©2021 Various Authors

DORA & KIKI
Publishing Company

HeartQuake

Table of Contents

HeartQuake

Heart:

Heart, the hollow muscular organ, which constitutes the motor center of the vertebrate circulatory system;

(fig.) center of man's emotional and spiritual life, therefore a symbol of his nature or behavior on the level of feelings, the intimacy of thought and feeling and affection or passion.

Earthquake:

Earthquake, vibratory movement of an area of the earth's surface;

(fig) upheaval, radical change.

It's a night like any other.

An instant and everything collapses, covering my body with rubble.

A night of forced immobility gives rise to an unstoppable stream of consciousness beyond space and the line of time.

A night of memories, imagination, and encounters, between what has been and what should have been, between time lost and time not yet lived, towards the leading destination, oneself.

An earthquake in the body and in the heart, which throws me in contact with my most intimate, frightened, and dark parts.

When everything seems over, when all hope seems useless, it is in that instant that, between the beating of the heart and the smooth sound of the breath, something begins to live.

A choice didn't kill me,

a new emotion,

nor a false step.

She killed me the fear of doing,

the security of the known,

the silent torment of the,

"I wish I did."

One step, one more,

before it remains only regret.

HeartQuake

Chapter I.

And Then It Was Darkness

00.23 am.

It all happened in a flash.

Sudden, ruthless.

A violent jolt that swept away every grip, every reference, every fixed point.

Everything that surrounded me covered me suddenly. Everything I owned, all the objects to which I tied myself, years of past life that I kept, now ended up depriving me of any possibility of movement. My body, motionless, under the rubble of what was once my home. My space now became my prison. Paradoxical.

And then I discovered something important. When everything is still and around is rubble and silence, when I cannot budge my steps, nor my hands, when everything seems to turn to the end, it is precisely there that something moves, arises, emerges in all its overflowing strength. My thoughts, my feelings.

My breath.

The slow sound of my heartbeat. The vital flow of my Being that breaks the boundaries of space and time and flies away, in every direction, in every age of mine, in every intersection between what has been, what could have been, and what hasn't happened.

There is something that nothing and no one can take away from me; my vital center that screams it exists.

The indomitable light of a beginning, when everything seems to be over.

What an illusion to think about we are in control.

What an illusion to think about we can defend ourselves from everything.

What an illusion.

My home.

I thought it was the safest place in the world.

It's the place that is about to become my grave.

The first few hours are just pain, that of the body, bones, and muscles. Every movement I try to make results in a discharge of painful bundles that cross my body.

The more I get upset, the more I get hurt. The more I do, the more pain I feel. I close my eyes in the dark.

Chapter II.
The Ghost of What Has Been

The first to visit me in the dark is a child. He has big eyes and messy blonde hair. He is wearing a white shirt with big red stripes and jeans-colored shorts. He is barefoot. He plays with his older brother on the sunny island of Ischia in mid-July. They collect black seeds from plants with bright pink flowers and use them as small projectiles to throw at them. He laughs, runs, and lies down on the floor when he gets hit. He gets dirty, but he doesn't care.

He laughs, throws his seeds, hides, lies down. There's nothing else in his eyes and his thoughts. It smells of the lightness that I have lost.

As a child, I was always in the sun.

The island of Ischia was all blue and green.

Harbor cranes were dinosaurs in my little games.

A path in the green, close to the beach, led to an abandoned farmhouse.

While walking along it, my brother and I had come across a group of children of our age, led by an older, or just taller, girl.

It was just her talking, and she described that path as a magical initiatory journey, and perhaps it was.

A magical path, full of wonders, which led to the castle of a woman with extraordinary powers.

We listened to her and followed her.

The blue of the sea in my eyes wide open, amazed at that new world.

I felt safe; my brother was always with me. We had the same clothes, in different colors.

Music. Far away. It arrives muffled as if I were underwater.

Far away, like the pain of the body. For a moment, it seems to have disappeared.

I beat time as if in a trance. And I move my toes.

Miett 'e creature 'o sol

pecché hanna sape'

addò fa fridd

e addò fa cchiù calore

[Pino Daniele]

"Put the children in the sun, because they need to know where it is cold and where it is warmest."

There can be no real awareness without experience, and perhaps not even true freedom.

Being able to choose presupposes having seen, discovered, experienced.

A. Jodorowsky writes, "birds kept in cages believe that flying is a disease."

Thanks, mom, thanks, dad. You have allowed me to experience the world and myself. You allowed me to fall, get up, find out. To create the foundation for me to become who I am.

Becoming a man is this. Breaking the bars of fear, breaking down walls, overcoming obstacles, moving your gaze, and steps beyond the rooms of the known.

You were given life.

And, with it, the silent prayer

to live it as best as possible.

Give it value.

Remember Who You Were

I was born tied to another person by a cord, then severed.

I cried, then I realized I could breathe.

Alone.

They fed me, washed me, dressed me, transported me.

My desire to discover has taken my first steps, slowly.

The first, shy steps, with the eyes fixed on my mother.

I was afraid.

I fell, I cried, I got up. Then, I stopped looking at her.

I was starting to trust my legs and my curiosity.

I explored, discovered, I was scared, amazed, I rejoiced and cried, I got hurt, I healed.

I have begun to choose.

The bonds to cultivate, the friendships and loves, the music to listen to, the passions and hobbies, the books to read.

I studied, I started a job, a relationship.

I have become, after so many years, what I am.

I, a person like the others, but unique and unrepeatable.

How much time, how much effort, how much beauty. Then, how could I allow a man, a woman, a parent, a broken love, a university professor, a social system, a job, an educational model, a television program, a computer, a smartphone, a social network to bring me back to a state of addiction?

How could I allow it the presumption of pretending to know what is right or wrong *for me*?

How could I allowed them to tell me what I want, what makes me feel good, what should I or shouldn't I do, say, choose, undertake?

It is *my life*, and I will build it however I want.

In a way that makes me happy. I choose to be free before anything else; before pleasing others, I respect my true self.

Over time, I have built my being a Person.

With every fall, cry, and rise.

I will defend it with all my strength.

I was born tied to another person by a cord, then severed.

And then a woman visits me.

It's you, Mom.

Your reassuring face, your smile.

That love of yours. You have been warmth and nourishment for me for nine months in your womb.

And then, to give me birth, you had to let me go.

How much did it cost you, how much did it cost me?

Cry and terror in that cut of a cord of life.

But that's when I discovered I could breathe with my lungs.

I am alive. I am me.

Love is holding. Love is letting go.

How many hours have I been down here? Today the pain is severe.

I don't hear music today.

Today it is only despair.

Today is the desire to surrender and fall into the dark.

No.

Remember Who You Are

So, breathe. Yes, breathe.

Breathe when you feel short of air, when the hours will weigh like the rubble of a shattered life.

Breathe when the crying clears your eyes, giving new light to your gazes on the world.

Breathe when anger burns your hands and thoughts, when you feel it's useless, when you think you won't be able to.

Breathe when fear blocks your legs and gestures and when the corners of new horizons open up to your senses.

Don't be afraid; it's just life flowing. Breathe.

There, in that rhythmic and constant movement, the center of your Being-there is enclosed.

Here, still and always.

It was a breath that conceived you.

It was a breath that pushed you into the light.

It was a breath that started that cry that, as soon as it arose, broke a bond and restored you to being a Person.

Breathe, you are alive. And nothing else matters.

" But from these deep wounds, free butterflies will come out
"[Alda Merini]

Remember me.

When everything feels like pain and fatigue and the darkness around will block your legs and choke your breath.

Remember me.

Of that hand stretched out in the darkness, when everything seemed to be fell apart in a night that you thought had no end.

Remember me.

Of my calm voice, to remind you of your breathing, your being alive, to give strength to your first slow step towards the dawn of a new day. And it was dawn, and it was a new day.

Remember, always remember me.

Of that time when you cried in despair, and I was there with you to let the tears flow, to wash away the pain, to admire your eyes, now shiny, big, alive.

Remember me.

Of when fear blocked your gestures and words, for that step so important to you, and you kept saying not to make it, and my voice whispered to you that no, it wasn't true, and to trust, and to go, go forward, without fear. And you let yourself go, and you did it.

Remember me.

Of my loving you always. Of my tender eyes admiring you naked, in the mirror. Love in my eyes, on your expressions, on your years, on your everyday gestures.

Remember.

Of my hands placed on your heart, reminding your courage, the regular sound of your being in the world, of your being Alive, of your being here.

Here I am. With you, once again, still and always. Remember me.

With love,

Yourself.

Chapter III

The Ghost of the Fear of Being

A nd then a man appears in the dark. He looks at me, looking out the window of his house. Flawless in his dark suit. He ironed shirt, shiny shoes, waistcoat. Hair perfectly pulled back.

He has an almost impassive expression. His movements are slow, as measured. Almost fearful.

He looks at me with a terrified expression.

"You can't die in your own home," he tells me. "No, you can't die in your own home."

"Shall We Try?"

That's what I have done, a whole life. Stand there, motionless, observing my choices from above. Tormented, but safe. From the window of my house. When I was still deceiving myself that staying still meant keeping me safe. Before realizing that the pile of choices not made, situations not lived, roads not traveled, emotions suffocated and tightened in cobwebs of ancient fears would have fallen on my stomach to weigh down my breath.

So, immobile.

Watching others go by, situations fading, life exhausting slowly, like a candle that brightens but does not illuminate, waiting for the excuse of that—too late—to which I would have clung to as if to a buoy, in the exhausting effort of staying afloat in my days.

From there, from that window, haunting my thoughts among the imagined scenarios of which was the right choice. But, no matter how hard I tried, my gaze stopped at that curve, there at the end of the road: what would I find next? Would I regret it? Would the other way have been better?

And, in the meantime, time passed.

It was there that I encountered the embarrassing truth of my limitations.

I was looking for impossible truths to hide the fear of a decision from myself.

There were no answers to those questions of mine. No right or wrong was stable or absolute. Human evaluations, these, linked to a specific time and moment. And an infinity of possible perspectives that confused me.

Here.

It would have been time to let me find out.

My legs would have shown me the way, step by step, discovery after discovery, emotion after emotion.

I looked down and read that writing on the asphalt. "Shall we try?"

A reassuring and steady voice, I could hear it coming from the deep silences of my Being.

And then I tried.

I stopped watching from above and finally went out onto the field.

And I left the house.

My existence was at stake, the profound meaning of my being in the world.

I took a step, another, and finally chose.

To get dirty, get excited, make mistakes, smile, suffer, fall, get up and start again.

I am finally alive, not only in thoughts but in my hands, in my feet, in my belly, and in my eyes.

I am finally alive, in all of myself.

How much happiness

you are giving up

for your need for

safety?

Out of the known,

there is a world

and part of you

all yet to discover.

Who am I? Who have I been? What do others see of me? What do I see? What part of me do I identify with?

My choices? My mistakes? My job? My goals?

I'm not this for sure.

I'm not my past.

I'm not my failures, the ramblings of my thoughts, my inconsistencies. I'm not expectations about my tomorrow. I'm not my education. I'm not what my parents imagined for me when 'me' did not exist yet. I'm not the expectations of others, the faithful friend, the present husband, the blameless person, the one who never gets angry, the one who always has the right word.

I'm not the words told to me, whispered like fragrant feathers, or thrown at me like pointed arrows.

I am not the one who must always be there. I am not the work I do. I am not the thought of being wrong.

Because I am not all of this, and one cannot be wrong in what one is not.

I am this moment.

I am the breath that reminds me to be alive. I'm unique. I am the desire that animates my hands. I am the curiosity and the desire for life that moves my legs.

I am my eyes wide open on the world, the purity of emotion experienced as the first time, the curve of the smile that softens the face beyond tears.

I am the games of me as a child, my eyes, sleepy and open, waiting for a new dawn to tear through the black of a night that will have to end.

Here, alive and present, desire and breath. Still and always.

I want to get out of here.

I scream, but the dust scratches my throat. And it increases my thirst. I try to move, but every movement is frustration and pain.

I want to get out of here.

Sound of water, like a distant roar.

The river flowed rapidly at that point, and I stopped there to watch the water crashing against the larger rocks. It circled it, creating a moving circle that enveloped the stone. I tried to modify its shape, throwing stones to skim that almost perfect circle. I was ten years old.

I have always enjoyed watching the shape of the river.

It follows a path that is never straight but made up of curves and involutions. The river always flows following that path, hour after hour, day after day, year after year.

It is not always the best route, the shortest, or the most direct one. It often covers curves upon curves to overcome valleys and obstacles.

But it follows that because that is the path it traced at its origin and, today, comes as the one already marked, less tiring, more automatic.

It is not the best, but it is the most comfortable.

The only way to change its route is to put an obstacle, something that can stop the reflex of that flowing always regular.

At that point, something surprising and special happens; *the river*, under the pressure of water, *creates a new path*, the best possible. And it overcomes obstacles, traces new trajectories, and discovers new forms of being. Like my life or everyone's life.

Methodical paths, traced roads, comfort zones determine the predictability of actions and reactions that ultimately puts down and devalues the creativity of our Being. We don't always live our best paths.

Until an unexpected break event occurs and modifies the profound structure of our existence. And then the change. If we stop resisting, is a natural process, which paints new possible scenarios for us.

And, like water, we can just follow it.

Confidently surrender to something bigger, benevolent, and wise: life.

Relax tense muscles, breathe deeply. Let loose.

Let Yourself Flow

And then I would stop kicking, getting angry, fighting.

It was not a surrender but a conscious decision to abandon my illusion of controlling the natural flow of events. Acceptance, they called it. I stopped.

And, suddenly, the edges of my face softened.

I was breathing.

I could hear the sound of the wind crossing my spaces, flowing with my thoughts, now no longer tense.

Something or someone was moving away from me, my anger, frustration, what had been and what should have been. All tension slipped away, like something so natural. I accompanied it with my eyes. It was a moment; I welcomed with gratitude.

Everything was free to go with its flow.

And I wasn't struggling anymore, but I was part of the entire flow of the universe. A voice, mine, stopped screaming and joined the melodious chorus of Existing. I flowed, harmony and breath.

Everything was free. And there was no more pain.

Get back to Essence.

One step back, to move forward.

Paradoxical, yes.

But the first step to finding our balance is a step back.

Going back, to go forward.

And I only realize it now that I'm trapped here, in this enforced stillness.

The logic of doing is the trap of our malaise. Too many commitments, tensions, displacements, schedules, tasks. Everything seems to have become vital, and it is precisely that which often takes us away from the truest vitality.

Far away.

Light years away from the essence of our pure flow, what we lived as children, for those children who were lucky enough to be.

We overestimate the mind. We overestimate the thought, the concept of—right or wrong—, the sense of guilt, the responsibility towards the judgment of others, the accumulation of doing. But our most vital and precious center, the fulcrum of our balance and well-being, is light years away from the ruminations of our mind. The human brain, as we know it today, is a rather modern acquisition, like a fruit on a tree that was born only because the roots drew the right nourishment. And our roots are not the labyrinths of our thoughts. I am not the commitments, I am not the job, I am not the others' judgment, the beautiful appearances, the designer clothes, the clean and perfect house.

Our roots are our breath, our steps in the world, the curiosity to discover, human bonds, meeting and letting go, knowing how to give and receive, dedicating time to ourselves, having fun, laughing and crying, loving.

All that I cannot do now and that I desperately wish I could.

So, I take a step back.

I walk away, slow down this rush of thoughts, and return to myself.

Chapter IV

The Ghost of Others' Expectations

And then a girl appears. She's well dressed, hair gathered in a braid, floral skirt, a handbag in her hands. She has a sweet, accommodating expression. She smiles, but her gaze betrays a hint of sadness.

She says she got married to her first love, a high school classmate, after years of dating. She has two children, Elisa and Andrea, and a husband who today seems to no longer see her beauty.

She tells of betrayals received, of words and tears that she had to swallow over time, and which ended up turning off the light that accompanied her smile in her eyes.

She says, "Because that's how it's done, that's how they taught me. Swallow, and go on, always. The family is renunciation, is sacrifice."

"Freedom costs and I'm afraid of loneliness. I don't know how I would do it alone. I've always had someone next to me, someone to lean on, to depend on, but who has ended up making me feel the worst kind of loneliness; the one that can be experienced in two".

I look at her, and I would like to hold her. I would like to tell her that only those who experiment, those who get involved, can really know their limits and resources. And the results are often surprising. You get to be amazed at your ability to change and recover.

Resilience, they call it. That all-human ability to overcome difficult situations and always get back on top again.

To be happy, you have to be disobedient. Whether it's towards a father, a mother, a partner, a family or social system, a limiting belief, the internal and self-sabotaging voice of—you can't do it—.

The road to self-fulfillment will always be paved with refusal and obstacles. But those who hinder you are often voicing their fears before your happiness. Whatever you choose to do, there will always be someone who will criticize you in some way.

But criticism from others is not a blow to your self-esteem if you don't allow it.

The new frightens, the change frightens, the feeling of losing control over the other frightens. Those who criticize or put you down are not better than you, nor safer, but they are certainly more limited and closed by their fears.

Making themselves great is the last answer of those who feel small.

—"Make mistakes always on your own"

—"Is this how gentlemen do it, grandma?"

—"This is how people

who want to be happy do it"

[From the movie Loose Cannons, by F. Ozpetek]

Say no, my dear, learn how to do it.

Because blind acceptance of others' expectations will always make you unhappy.

It's your life, and it's up to you to make it the way you want it.

Disobedience is growth.

So, say it. You do not want to, that you disagree, that you changed your mind, that it does not suit you.

Because a loud—no—is a—yes—you will whisper to yourself.

Only two letters, but a small big step towards the horizon of your wanting to be. So, just like you really are.

Maybe you will meet who you are only later.

Beyond the expectations of others.

When who you choose to be is no longer to fit into what you think is right, or what others, family, partner, society, and your roles expect of you.

Yourself, and that's okay.

Perhaps you will meet true Love only later.

Beyond your self-centered living.

When—I love you—is no longer just—I love how you make me feel, I love what you do for me—but—I love you—, I love the person that YOU are.

Different from my expectations, ideals, or projections.

Beyond all my fears.

Yourself, and that's okay.

So, just say it.

Enough of what they expect from me, enough to always want me the same, enough for my fears, enough to the sense of inadequacy that limits me; we are human, same and different, imperfect and unique. Enough of self-built cages, limitations given and received; I will be what I am, and I will love you for who you are.

Stop manipulations, heart's addictions, every moment I spent brooding on a past that is now gone, blind to the present and its new gifts.

No more complaints, no more defeatism, no more saying—I can't—.

I will always try, chasing my dreams, and if I fail, I will try again, in a new form.

I will open my eyes to my present, I will look people in the face and the new day, with respect and trust.

I will be the daily and surprising discovery of a new me.

Feet to the ground, look at the stars.

Cold. It is still night, scattered shouting, siren sounds in the distance.

I have a habit of never wearing pajamas. They will find me wearing sweatpants and a white T-shirt.

If they find me.

What strange jokes the mind makes. What an absurd thought to worry about this, now.

Naked, so I was born.

I didn't choose my first clothes; they chose them for me.

How much of me really belongs to me?

Habits, beliefs, ways of doing things, rules. Is what's right or wrong really for me?

If something makes me unhappy, why do I persist in keeping it?

If something makes me happy, why don't I run after it?

Perhaps rebirth is just that; letting go of many things, stripping off clothes that don't belong to me.

Naked, as I was born.

To later, finally, get dressed in me.

Chapter V

The Ghost of What Has Not Been

The man who visits me now worries me. He is dressed in black, his eyes are half-closed, his nails worn out by the continuous digging of him. Yes, he digs, always looking for something. He does it relentlessly.

He almost seems not to notice what surrounds him, the colors of the world, what his eyes look at, his feet trampling the ground. He appears to float. Lost, in a continuous elsewhere. Thus, in mid-air, as if he were everywhere and nowhere.

His pockets are full of glittering stones. Colorful and precious. Gems, which he believes are pieces of glass.

He does not look at them. He does not care.

He seeks, keeps seeking.

"What are you looking for?" I ask him.

He does not even look up, and with a faint voice, he replies,

"I'm looking for what has not been."

That love over, that train not taken, that choice not made.

The echo of the lost possibilities that resounds in our Today.

The voice of unlived life that overwhelmingly bursts, taking energy away from the life we live.

How strange to get lost in what has not been.

What a strange thing, always imagining it as a bright option to what is real today.

It would have been nicer.

I would have been happier.

I would have done all those things.

It would have been the love of my life.

The truth is that each moment is the child of an unrepeatable combination of innumerable factors. Our existence itself is.

A minute late, and your great grandparents might not have met. And you wouldn't be here, maybe.

Those forgotten keys, you searching for them and wasting those moments to leave the house may have saved your life, and you cannot know it.

That former love could have turned into hell.

That train not taken could have led you to a life of misery.

We do not know. We cannot know.

It is useless to get lost in the maze of lost possibilities.

It has not been. It couldn't be.

The real miracle is that you are here.

And this certainly deserves your attention.

Learn to love your home scent before opening the door and searching for the ones of the world.

Because nothing, nothing is taken for granted. Everything is a gift.

Breathe, you are alive.

Give your Now the value it deserves.

What's past is past.

Let it go.

Today can be the beginning of a new tomorrow.

A first step that will turn into a journey, if you want.

Make your past, what you build every day from now on, become something to smile about.

How can I smile at a path that is now not a path? How can I smile at this darkness, this stillness, this silence, this body that aches, the thirst, the hunger, this life that cannot and must not end like this?

And then a sudden memory.

A university professor (I was a student in the early years of psychology, and I don't remember his name anymore) that day began his lesson by singing these words, taken from a well-known classic Neapolitan song;

Dicitencello

a 'sta cumpagna vosta

Ch'aggio perduto

'o suonno e 'a fantasia

Ch a penzo sempe

Ch'è tutt a vita mia

[Dicitencello vuje, Fusco – Falvo, 1930]

"Tell this friend of yours, I've lost sleep and fantasy. That I always think of her, that she is my whole life."

"And no, dear boys", he added.

"You can lose your money, you can even shed tears, you lose weight and appetite, you can lose sleep, but never ever," he said in a sharp and firm voice, "allow someone, anything to take your fantasy, imagination, desire."

So, keep going, keep desiring, always.

Because desire is the cornerstone of any construction.

Something to start with, something to take care of, something to grow.

Now, at this moment, when everything is dark.

Tomorrow, when the dawn will sweep away all gloomy thoughts.

Always, in every awakening of your life.

And if your dream is far away, dream harder.

There is no distance for a heart that desires.

And then green meadows, my bare feet on the grass, a slice of pizza eaten looking at the sea, her and her funny faces, my father smiling, my mother's good morning on holidays, laughter with my brothers, the sweetness of my grandmother to hug again.

It will soon be dawn.

HeartQuake

Chapter VI

The Ghost of Happiness

Seeking happiness outside of us

it's like waiting for the sun to rise

in a cave facing north.

(Tibetan adage)

The man who now appears to me in the dark is immobile.

Seated, he makes no sound other than his breathing. A calm and regular breath, listening to him is almost hypnotic. I feel my body relax in the cyclical nature of his inhalations and exhalations.

He tells of having been a wealthy merchant, having traveled the world in every part of him searching for the most precious and attractive goods to resell. He has amassed a fortune in a few decades.

Then one day, following investments that proved unsuccessful, he found himself losing most of the money he had accumulated and fell into the darkest despair. His greed alienated him from his old friends, and he sacrificed family, love to pursue his riches.

He was alone, incredibly alone.

One day he was sitting on a bench in a park tormenting his fingers and thoughts, and an unexpected scene came to his eyes. A small rubber ball, bright yellow, crosses the field of vision and stops a few inches from his left foot. A minute passes, then two, then five, and then a man appears, followed by a crying child. The man grabs the ball, hands it to the child that immediately stops crying, then smiles and hugs that man, and then they both smile.

It is said that it was there at the top.

She is hidden in a cave with silver reflections.

Motionless, in eternal waiting, accessible to those brave or reckless few willing to leave their homes and explore the borders of the new world.

It is said that it was of blinding splendor. Eternal, immortal, motionless in its silent casket, up there, far from man and the noises of the world. Although many have set out in search of it, it seems that no one has ever managed to find it. The first time I heard of it was on Christmas day. Sitting on the carpet, surrounded by torn wrapping papers, people, and flashing lights. I was holding a white teddy bear in my hands, with earthy ears and a nose as black as coal.

"Look at him. He is so happy", my mother said to who knows who.

So it was that I learned the name of that strange sensation that ran through me; excitement, discovery, euphoria.

Was it like that, then? Sudden and sweetly violent, after waiting for midnight and tear the paper off the presents.

Happiness.

And then I think that

if there is happiness, it is because there was waiting,

if there is happiness, it is because there was desire,

if there is happiness, it is because there was first frustration or boredom,

if there is happiness, it is because there was love.

Happiness is an internal state, made up of small things to which we choose to give importance; the unexpected smile of a stranger, the clear gaze to observe the sunrise after a rainy night, a forgotten note that suddenly appears from the pocket of an old coat, a small yellow rubber ball found.

Wanting everything at once means missing everything, and no happiness in the world is not born from an act of love.

No. It is another of those moments.

Of those in which the numbness of the body becomes a shell of dark thoughts. It will end, I've been telling myself for too long, but the only thing that seems to end is my strength and my patience.

I must have read somewhere that colors don't exist. Yes, they don't. They are none other than the refraction of the objects of part of the chromatic spectrum. If they reflect it all, they appear white.

If they absorb it all, then black.

If only part of it is reflected, they appear the color we perceive.

The world is in black and white. Light caresses it giving it color.

Incredible. And then I wonder why on earth I can't do the same now. Give color. Maybe it's all gray around because my thoughts are gray.

We look at the world from a window, but perhaps the world is a mirror; it reflects what we contain.

The pain you feel is a crossroads of possibilities.

A juncture.

One way is victimization, feeling sorry for yourself, blaming others, or cursing the world.

The other is an opportunity for change. Roll up your sleeves, rediscover your strength, make a choice.

And start over. You have heart, courage.

You must be happy Now.

Before any strategy or reasoning, before the mortgage on your happiness becomes the structure of endless self-deception. Something will not come if you do not do it.

And therefore, not yesterday, not tomorrow, not the others, not the circumstances or the right moment. Stop waiting or losing yourself in excuses you believe in less every day.

Now

That's all you have for sure

that's all you need for sure.

Each flight begins with a jump.

What time is it? How much time did I spend down here?

Can a night never end?

Once I read a Zen story. The story was about a king who commissioned a ring from the most famous goldsmith in the kingdom.

He asked him to engrave a secret sentence that he would have read exclusively in a moment of extreme difficulty to lift up when everything seemed to turn towards the darkest despair.

And so he did. He wore the ring for years and, one day, during a bloody battle, when he was now cornered, wounded, exhausted, without strength, he took it off and read the sentence inside for the first time: *even this moment will pass.*

It left me blown away. What apparently is a banal sentence, is actually one of the greatest truths of existence; everything passes. Every phase, every sorrow, every joy, every pain, every difficult moment.

It is the natural cycle of events.

Every summer turns into autumn, every winter into spring, every darkness towards the light.

The king's battle ended.

I close my eyes and smile.

Even this moment will pass.

Chapter VII

The Ghost of Time

Then a woman appears; she is about forty years old. Thin legs, nervous hands, a red dress that contrasts with a black overcoat, her skin is clear, her eyes tired.

She moves her feet continuously, shifting the balance of her body from one side to the other. Her movements are not very soft, with sudden jerks.

She transmits all the restlessness that she contains.

After a time that seems infinitely long, she begins to speak.

She says she always did everything that had to be done in the times when it had to be done. She met her current husband at university when she was twenty. At twenty-five, she graduated, and after a few months, she found a job, and the following year she got married. She bought a small but cute house with a mortgage, furnished it like the house she always wanted. She had her first child after just over a year of marriage, a girl, Sara. And after two years, the second, a boy, Alessandro.

A perfect life.

In perfect times.

She was the pride of his father and mother, impeccable woman, worker, wife, and mother.

A few days ago, she turned forty.

She was there, in front of the candles to blow out, in the soft light of her living room, surrounded by family and friends to wish her a happy birthday.

"Happy birthday to you."

And then a second of silence. The flickering light of the flames, her breath to turn them off in a single breath.

A moment, and then darkness.

She says she felt a strange sensation in her stomach. A void, a black hole. Something unsettling, incomprehensible, and frightening.

For a moment, she looked at her hands, she felt them tremble but they were still.

And a question to creep into her gaze between the lines of her mascara;

"And now?"

She says she has always identified her life with doing, with the achievement of what for her were the proper steps, the right goals.

As if her life were a marathon, marked by kilometers to be covered at the fair times.

The life.

The unfathomable, labyrinthine life, enclosed in the forced scheme of a program to follow. Coupons to earn for who knows what reward.

Doing, running, even before learning to stay.

Stop, breathe, feel.

"Life is short. We cannot stop. Never."

I ran, ran, ran, ran.

Among the folds of the hours, on the back of my days.

I didn't stop. I didn't turn around.

I ran, ran, ran, ran.

Because it's right, because that's how it's done.

I've been running all my life. I've been running all the time.

I've always been running.

I took everything. I kept everything of mine.

And then I arrived.

Before all and everything.

I turned around, and I didn't find myself.

I got there first.

Before myself.

Before my happiness.

And in a moment, just as it arrived, it disappears.

When I travel, I have the feeling that time is expanding dramatically.

Three days, which in my daily life are nothing, seem to cover an infinite time, a full-time, rich. When I get into bed in the evening, my legs are tired, and my eyes are full of endless images of the day just passed.

A feeling of infinite fullness.

I think it is due to what happens when you visit a new place; every habit falls. Everything has to be experienced and discovered. Streets, habits, where and what to eat, colors, scents, sounds. The senses work at maximum frequency. You feel to be fully immersed, moment by moment, in what you are experiencing.

Habits, a cross to bear but also a delight. So reassuring, they allow you to surround yourself with a muffled feeling of familiarity and security, but better not to abuse it.

The same things, the same people, the same dynamics, the same places. Reassuring, but it is like living in one of those glass spheres with snow. Without knowing or wondering what is out there.

And there is a whole world outside.

A whole life.

Experiences, sensations, emotions. It is time to experience them.

Listen, girl.

This life is not short, and this life is not long.

This life is short if you choose to live it within the perimeters of the known; the same habits, places, people.

This life is long if you don't stop discovering, believing in it, getting excited, getting to know new places, new people, new habits, new risks, new achievements.

How much of your life are you choosing to live?

You have the time you need.

It's up to you to put it to good use.

So:

Fall, but then get up.

Get angry, but then forgive.

Get lost, but then find yourself.

Grow up, but then become a child again.

Join, but then separate.

Cry, but then smile again.

Start, but then learn to finish.

Collect, but then open up to the world.

Move your steps, but then learn to stop.

Love, and then hate, but then love again, and again, and again.

Because life is movement,

because change is necessary,

because there is no expression of your potential that you cannot experience.

But Love is the center of your Being, always.

Stop.

Breathe.

Live this moment with all of yourself.

In a few years, you will turn around and remember it with regret.

You almost did not notice it, so lost in the search for a continuous elsewhere.

You will close your eyes, and a sigh will slowly lift your chest.

And then you will give it a name.

You will call it; happiness.

Live now. That's all that matters.

Chapter VIII
The Ghost of the Right Thing

And then a woman appears. Big black eyes, hair tied in a long ponytail, pleated skirt, collegiate look. She is sitting composed, her small hands gathered together on her knees, back straight. Her body sways almost imperceptibly back and forth as if struggling to find the center of gravity of a point of balance between two different positions, the *straight* one and the *comfortable* one.

She talks about having desires that she shouldn't have. Because they are not fair, not adequate, not in line with her age, and with her role as mother and wife. She met a man by chance, and she suddenly felt the awakening of feelings and emotions that had been dormant for many, too many years of repetitiveness. "I should never have met him", she says, "I feel like a teenager". She talks about that sudden encounter, with eyes full of light and hands discharging sudden energy. She seems to like what she feels. "But no, I shouldn't feel it", she stresses right away.

Feeling a vital, full push, and suffocating is exhausting. It requires a tremendous energy effort. It is like taking a part of yourself and deciding to cut it clean.

Pleasure, the natural tension towards a desire, sacrificed to respect what needs to be done, what—The Right Thing—represents.

This is how, day by day, we kill parts of us.

Vital parts, energetic parts, which we suffocate under the weight of a ton of ideas—mostly not ours but acquired—*of how to live*. A kind of existence etiquette that no one has ever written but everyone respects. Everything in its place and time, even our emotions.

I would like to tell her to listen to herself before censoring herself.

Nothing happens by mistake in the flow of our existence, even profound and unsettling changes.

Every human being has infinite parts within him. We are often unaware until they emerge, with their overflowing strength. And they do so to make themselves known, to make us known. Jolts of our ego come close to what we must become aware of in that particular moment of our existence.

No part of us is our enemy.

Come on girl, open your eyes, your senses, your heart.

Let the wind blow into the rooms of your emotions.

The senses are made to perceive, the feelings to feel, the heart to beat. Do not worry.

There is more life between scattered sheets and a bit of disorder than in a dark and dusty room.

And if they criticize you, know that no one can blame you for following your heart.

Criticism is often the voice of those who always want you the same because they are afraid or of those who feel secret envy for your courage to let you flow.

Your emotions, your dreams, are your responsibility, your little treasure that is up to you to decide whether to feed or let it die. One day you will be the only spectator and judge of your choices.

Value your desires. They are the purest and most vital part of your Being.

Give yourself madness every so often. Listen to yourself, let yourself flow, come on.

Sometimes what we call madness is nothing but life going beyond the boundaries that we have given ourselves or that we have been given. Rebellious and precious glimpses of messy identity. A life that does not allow itself to be limited.

The silent voice screams that you can be so much more than you wanted to believe.

And then faces, the women I've loved, the houses I've lived in, the places I've frequented, the habits I've changed. How many lifetimes have I gone through? Parenthesis of life kept inside one in the other like Chinese boxes.

Our existence is full of meetings and greetings, of beginnings and closings.

As many lives, how many we will decide to live.

What is left to connect the meaning of existence? My memories, the sense of my being there.

I, the only witness to the continuity of my years.

I will choose to experience them all, in joy and pain, in health and sickness, when the sun is high and on a cold and dark night like this. A marriage with myself, before with others.

Life is basically this, a colorful carousel of unrepeatable moments.

Beautiful and ugly, fast or slow, angry and calm, still or stormy, passionate and tender.

Careless details, frequently ignored, taken for granted, mortified, or crushed by the neurotic marathon of our commitments. Each of those moments, colored by the absolute, embodies the deepest meaning of our being in the world.

So precious.

So, I choose to live them because life is all here; wonderful game, end and a new beginning, thrill of discovery, caress of the evening, warm hug that comforts and refreshes.

I stop chasing the image of eternal happiness, and I learn to bless the storms of my days; one day,

I will call them the life that I will have lived.

There is more beauty in a valley that lights up after the rain than in a desert blinded by a perennial sun.

> *"There is snow in my memories*
>
> *There is always snow*
>
> *And my brain goes white if I don't stop remembering.*
>
> *Down here, nothing is a sin. And if you ask me if I would do it all again I tell you, 'Yes, it was worth it'."*
>
> *[From the movie Love Manual 2].*

To live, I ask nothing more, and I will do nothing but live.

To live, to let myself go to this wonderful and a little crazy flow that is life.

Follow it, with respectful touch and wonder in my eyes, like a child.

Without fear, but with heart and trust.

Abandon me, listen to my breath, open senses and heart, feel before thinking.

So that one day I too can say that—yes, it was worth it—.

My dear, amid hatred I found that there was in me

an invincible love.

Amid tears

I found that there was in me

an invincible smile.

Amid chaos

I found that there was in me invincible tranquility.

Finally, I understood that in the middle of winter,

I found that there was in me an invincible summer.

And that it makes me happy.

Because it says it doesn't matter how hard the world go
against me, there is something stronger in me, something
better that immediately pushes me back.

(Albert Camus)

And then I realized something very, very important.

The difficulties, the falls, the defeats, that pain, and all the difficult moments in my history were no interruptions to my existence.

They were not spaces of non-life, which punctuated the moments that I defined—happy—, happiness which, among other things, acquired substance precisely because of those intervals.

They were life, growth, the margins of my new paths. They were the cornerstone of the life path. They were springboards, they were changes, they were sprouts of a new equilibrium.

I stopped resisting or suffocating them, and I learned to welcome them. I stopped waiting and started living.

No night did not see its dawn.

I woke up. I opened my eyes to a new day.

My lungs filled with the morning air.

I was alive. I was now.

I took a step and went to meet my present.

Chapter IX
The Ghost of What Will Be

And then a vision; a child, messy hair, big, lively eyes. He reaches out a hand in my direction, he looks at me, in his gaze, there is the sense of the continuity of a whole life, mine. He holds a white teddy bear in his hands, with earth-colored ears and a nose as black as coal. He smiles lightly at his happiness.

It was a moment.

The gentle touch of that baby me.

Those moments of happiness that I would have chosen to live and give to the world. The deeper meaning of living; doing, offering, and giving oneself, welcoming and discovering, waiting and desiring.

The extraordinary strength of all the charcoal-nosed bears that were there, waiting for me, if only I wanted and knew how to recognize them, get to know them, live them. That treasure, so long pursued, no longer hidden in the secret hideouts of legendary caves but revealed and alive there, at the center of my desires and gestures.

Of my opening my heart to the world and to others; that treasure of mine, my happiness that depended only on me. Like a bud that needs water and light to blossom and reveal itself in all its perfumed beauty.

I felt the blood throbbing in my veins and surprising energy flowing through the fibers of my body, vitalizing muscles, bones, and senses.

My legs, now I can move them.

This moment is my whole life;

everything that has been, that I have lived, that should have been, the climbs and hills of my days, my moments of happiness, my desires. The end and the beginning, the extremes of a continuum condensed in the space of an instant, this instant.

Now is the time.

A breath, a sudden effort, the rotation of my body under kilograms of rubble that gives new spaces to my movements. Yes, I move, I can move, I don't feel pain, but the strength of a breath that screams is enough, that screams now, that screams life, life to live.

I am lying, now prone. From this spot, I can perceive bright glimpses beyond the darkness of what has been.

Of course, I'll hurt you.

Of course, you'll hurt me.

Of course, we will hurt each other.

But this is the very condition of existence.

To become spring means accepting the risk of winter.

To become a presence means accepting the risk of absence...

(The Little Prince, A. De Saint-Exupery)

Flashes of light. I look at my watch. It marks 6.40. It is already morning.

It feels like a beautiful clear day, with no clouds. I observe a strip of the sky from my field of view limited by the weight of what it was. It is clear, of an intense blue, and with a hint of wonder, I see it; the moon, there, a few edges above the horizon line.

When it is night, it is night for us.

When it's summer, it's summer for us.

Our dichotomous vision (white or black) always pushes us towards a sectorial vision, often to the detriment of the other party who, when it emerges, amazes, despairs, terrifies us.

When it is daytime, the moon is still there in the sky.

When it's summer here, the other half of the earth is experiencing its winter.

I'm not all good, all strong. Not my partner, my parents, not my friends are. I can't always be happy or always sad.

Each thing, each phase, always holds the other part within itself.

It is so for joy or sadness, beauty, suffering, purity, success, defeat, hatred, or love.

It is so for this moment.

So, I watch that moon to remind me that even this rising day will have a night and that in these early autumn hours, there is a place, never too far away, that blooms with the scent of its early spring.

Prone, my arms sweeping away the remains of what was once a desk, my desk. A push with the hands to slip away from these spaces. And I slide, and I move, slow and inexorable. I gain inches of freedom.

A moment throughout my life. The air, fresh and clean air from my nostrils, flows into my body. It smells new, it smells of a beginning, it smells of a tomorrow that is now today.

It was an instant. I breathed relentlessly, reaching the top of the most challenging and essential mountain of my life. My eyes open to admire the scenery of dawn that swept away the blackness of a night that seemed to never end.

Here I am, still alive.

A look back to not forget where I was.

A look at my feet to show me the truth of being here and now.

A look ahead to remind me that, as long as my heart beats, nothing is really lost and anything can still happen.

I turned and saw them. What has been, the fear of being, what others expect, what has not been, time, and the right thing.

A child, three women, and two men; were the ghosts that accompanied my night.

They moved away from my field of vision, walking slowly, holding hands, until they disappeared along the horizon line now illuminated by the first rays.

I felt my heart tighten.

I greeted them with gratitude. I knew I would never see them again.

I looked down, and there it was; the bear with the charcoal nose, the ghost of my happiness. Still and always, with me.

I pressed him to my heart in tears of emotion.

I felt my face light up the darkness of my no longer tense muscles with a smile.

And then there was Light.

.

Chapter X.
Of the End and the Beginning

It is when you realize the finitude of your existence that you really begin to live.Finitude is a strange word. It has two meanings; being finite, complete, that is, brought to completion, therefore perfect. And being finite, in the sense of limited, that is, imperfect. A single term that contains two apparently diametrically opposed meanings; perfection and imperfection, completeness and limitation.

What is perfect or accomplished is limited.

What is limited, unfinished, is perfect.

A single word that masterfully encloses the profound meaning of human existence; perfect and imperfect, complete and unfinished.

The completeness of a life that substantiates its own limitation.

Like my life, like yours, like everyone's life.

It is when you realize the finitude of your existence that you really begin to live.

The end that gives birth to the beginning.

The light that rises, after a night that seemed to have no end.

And now that my eyes are open, that I move my hands, that my legs respond to the desire to move, transforming my desires into real places and faces, I realize how lucky I am.

That was close that all this was not.

And now that it is daytime, consider this book as palindrome words; that have the particularity to be read from one side to another, without changing their meaning.

From beginning to end or from end to beginning.

And then it was the light after the dark.

And then it was dark, after the light.

Nobody escapes the laws of life.

It is between these two extremes that the profound sense of your being there is enclosed.

Moment by moment, breath by breath.

Drop your thoughts and move your steps.

Follow, and don't be afraid.

You cannot know where they will take you.

Where, how, with whom.

Living is a journey of discovery.

But one thing is sure.

When the journey is moved by the coordinates of the heart, the goal will never be far from the center of your very Essence.

There, in the center of you.

Nothing is taken for granted, and every day is a precious gift.
Give it the value it deserves.

A new dawn spreads out
glimmers of light to my eyes
Words to the lips
Caresses to the hands
Paths at my feet.
And so I observe,
and so I say,
and so I go,
and so I love.
Forgive me, oh far night,
you that make the moments golden,
and donate awakening:
I shall welcome you
when it's your time.
But now it's day,
and I breathe,
and my heart beats.

And I live.

www.ingramcontent.com/pod-product-compliance
Lightning Source LLC
Chambersburg PA
CBHW030302030426
42336CB00009B/490